ADVANCED OXYGEN THERAPY

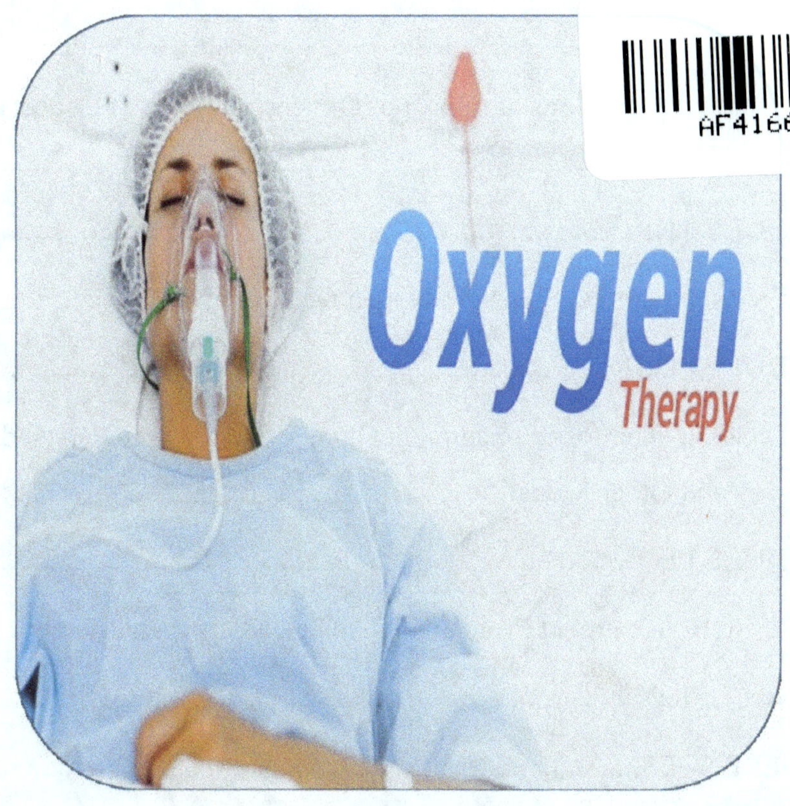

TABLE OF CONTENTS

INTRODUCTION

Oxygen therapy has been a cornerstone in the treatment of various respiratory conditions and critical care situations. As healthcare providers whether respiratory therapists, doctors, or nurses understanding the complex dynamics of oxygen therapy can make the difference between life and death for patients. Despite being one of the most frequently administered medical therapies, the advanced principles of oxygen therapy are often underappreciated or misunderstood. This book, "Mastering Advanced Oxygen Therapy: A Comprehensive Guide for Healthcare Providers," is designed to serve as a detailed, practical, and engaging resource for healthcare professionals who wish to deepen their understanding of oxygen therapy beyond the basics.

Oxygen therapy is not just about delivering oxygen; it's about doing so in the most effective, safe, and precise manner for each individual patient. This guide delves into the foundations of oxygen transport, exploring the physiological mechanisms that govern how oxygen is carried in the blood and how tissues utilize it. As we progress through the lesson, we'll look closely at clinical signs that indicate oxygen deficiency (hypoxia) or excess (hyperoxia), as well as the subtle signs of imbalance that can complicate patient outcomes.

A crucial aspect of advanced oxygen therapy is its diagnostic and imaging correlations. Healthcare providers must learn to recognize the impact of oxygen therapy on diagnostic imaging, such as X-rays, and interpret changes in lung architecture or other physiological structures that arise from oxygen therapy. Moreover, we explore the pharmacological aspect of oxygen therapy, detailing medications that complement oxygen administration, including bronchodilators, corticosteroids, and sedatives used in ventilatory support. Understanding these drugs and their interaction with oxygen therapy is key to managing critically ill patients.

This book is an essential resource for those looking to advance their practice and provide high-quality care to patients requiring oxygen therapy, whether in acute care settings, critical care, or chronic respiratory management.

MODULE ONE

LESSON: UNDERSTANDING OXYGEN THERAPY

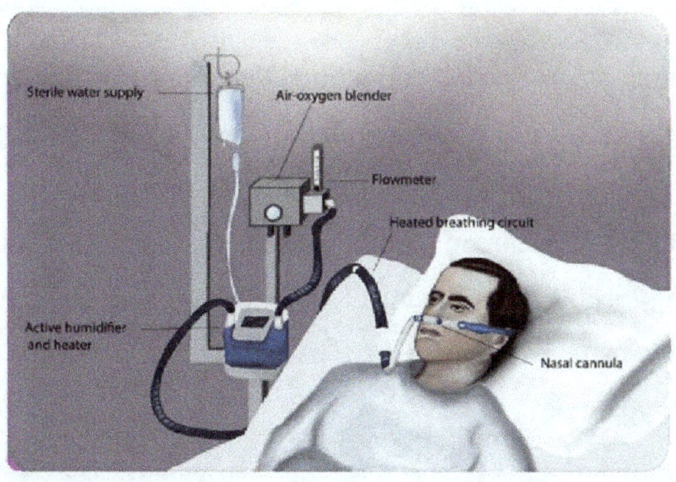

Oxygen therapy is one of the most frequently administered treatments in healthcare settings, ranging from emergency rooms and ICUs to outpatient clinics. It serves as a lifeline for patients suffering from various respiratory, cardiovascular, and metabolic conditions. However, understanding the foundational principles behind oxygen therapy is crucial for healthcare providers who wish to use it effectively. In this lesson, we will explore the science behind oxygen therapy, its indications, and the fundamental guidelines for its safe and effective use.

The Role of Oxygen in the Human Body

Oxygen is essential for cellular respiration, the process by which cells produce energy. Every tissue and organ in the human body depends on a continuous supply of oxygen to function properly. The absence of adequate oxygen known as hypoxia can lead to cellular damage, organ dysfunction, and eventually death if not corrected in a timely manner.

Oxygen therapy is aimed at correcting hypoxemia (low blood oxygen levels) by delivering supplemental oxygen to the patient. It is commonly used in conditions like chronic obstructive pulmonary disease (COPD), pneumonia, asthma exacerbations, heart failure, and in patients requiring mechanical ventilation. The objective is to restore adequate oxygenation to tissues without causing oxygen toxicity (hyperoxia).

Types of Oxygen Therapy

Low-flow oxygen systems: These include nasal cannula and simple face masks, providing oxygen concentrations of 24-60%. Low-flow systems are suitable for patients with mild to moderate hypoxia who can still breathe effectively on their own.

- High-flow oxygen systems: Venturi masks and non-rebreather masks are part of this category. High-flow systems can deliver oxygen concentrations close to 100% and are used for patients with severe hypoxia who require higher levels of oxygen.
- Mechanical ventilation: For critically ill patients, mechanical ventilation becomes necessary when the respiratory system cannot maintain adequate oxygenation or ventilation.

Ventilators can deliver controlled oxygen concentrations, pressures, and volumes, tailored to the patient's needs.

Indications for Oxygen Therapy

- The decision to initiate oxygen therapy is based on clinical signs of hypoxia and laboratory values, such as arterial blood gases (ABG) and pulse oximetry.

- Hypoxemia: When blood oxygen levels drop below 90% saturation on pulse oximetry, or PaO2 falls below 60 mm Hg in ABG, oxygen therapy is indicated.

- Tachypnea or Dyspnea: Rapid or difficult breathing is often a sign of respiratory distress, requiring immediate intervention with supplemental oxygen.

- Cyanosis: Bluish discoloration of the skin or mucous membranes, particularly the lips and fingers, indicates poor oxygenation.

- Altered Mental Status: Confusion, agitation, or unconsciousness in a patient with respiratory distress may be a sign of severe hypoxia.

Guidelines for Oxygen Therapy

Administering oxygen therapy should be based on the principle of providing the minimal amount of oxygen necessary to maintain adequate oxygen saturation (SpO2). The target saturation for most patients is between 92-96%, though for COPD patients, it may be lower, around 88-92%, to prevent hypercapnia (high levels of carbon dioxide).

Oxygen Toxicity and Hyperoxia

While oxygen is vital, excessive oxygen administration can cause harm, particularly in patients with chronic lung diseases or pre-existing hypercapnia. Prolonged exposure to high concentrations of oxygen can result in oxygen toxicity, leading to lung damage, increased oxidative stress, and complications such as absorption atelectasis. Therefore, it is important to monitor oxygen levels and adjust the delivery system accordingly.

MODULE TWO

LESSON: PHYSIOLOGICAL IMPACT OF OXYGEN: OXYGEN TRANSPORT AND UTILIZATION

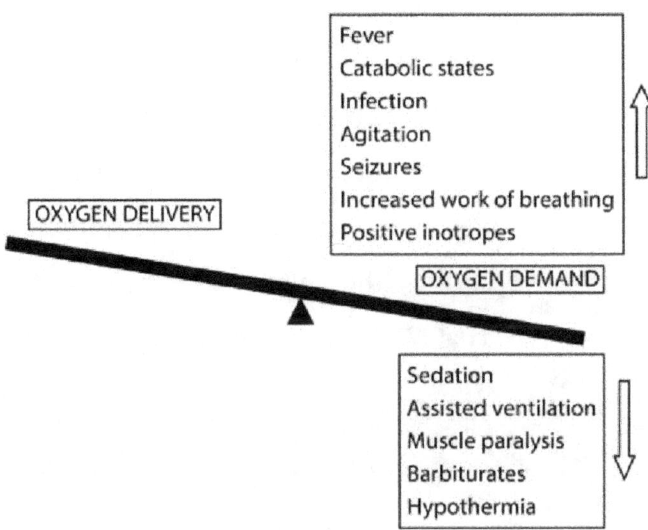

Oxygen is fundamental to human life, and the mechanisms through which it is transported and utilized in the body are complex and finely tuned. In this lesson, we will explore the physiology of oxygen transport, the role of hemoglobin, and the factors that influence oxygen delivery to tissues. Understanding these processes is key for healthcare providers administering oxygen therapy, as they must ensure that oxygen is delivered effectively without causing harm to patients.

Oxygen Transport in the Body

Oxygen enters the body through the respiratory system. Air is inhaled into the lungs, where oxygen diffuses into the bloodstream across the alveolar-capillary membrane. From there, oxygen is transported throughout the body, primarily bound to hemoglobin in red blood cells, and delivered to tissues where it is used for cellular respiration.

Role of Hemoglobin

Hemoglobin is a protein found in red blood cells responsible for carrying oxygen from the lungs to tissues and organs. Each molecule of hemoglobin can bind up to four molecules of oxygen. The oxygen-hemoglobin dissociation curve, a key concept in understanding oxygen transport, describes the relationship between the partial pressure of oxygen (PaO2) and the percentage of hemoglobin saturation (SpO2).

- Oxygen Saturation (SpO2): This refers to the percentage of hemoglobin molecules that are fully saturated with oxygen. Normal oxygen saturation ranges from 95% to 100% in healthy individuals.
- Partial Pressure of Oxygen (PaO2): PaO2 measures the amount of oxygen dissolved in the blood plasma and is expressed in millimeters of mercury (mm Hg). It reflects how much oxygen is available for diffusion into tissues.

The curve is sigmoidal (S-shaped), meaning that hemoglobin's affinity for oxygen increases as more oxygen molecules bind to it. However, at very high levels of oxygen saturation (above 90%), adding more oxygen to the bloodstream only results in minimal increases in hemoglobin saturation, as it approaches full capacity.

Conversely, at lower PaO2 levels, hemoglobin releases oxygen more readily to tissues in need.

Shifts in the Oxygen-Hemoglobin Dissociation Curve

Several physiological factors can shift the oxygen-hemoglobin dissociation curve, affecting hemoglobin's affinity for oxygen:

- Rightward Shift: Factors such as increased temperature, elevated levels of carbon dioxide (CO2), decreased pH (acidosis), and increased levels of 2,3-diphosphoglycerate (2,3-DPG) in red blood cells cause a rightward shift. This means hemoglobin has a lower affinity for oxygen, promoting oxygen release to tissues. This is beneficial during exercise or in states of increased metabolic demand, where tissues require more oxygen.

- Leftward Shift: Conversely, a leftward shift occurs with decreased temperature, lower CO2 levels, increased pH (alkalosis), or decreased 2,3-DPG levels. In this case, hemoglobin has a higher affinity for oxygen, meaning it holds onto oxygen more tightly and is less willing to release it to tissues. This can impair oxygen delivery to peripheral tissues, which may become problematic in critically ill patients.

Oxygen Utilization in Tissues

Once oxygen reaches the tissues, it is used by cells to produce energy in the form of adenosine triphosphate (ATP) through a process called cellular respiration. This process primarily occurs in the mitochondria, the powerhouse of the cell. The oxygen that enters cells is critical for aerobic metabolism, which is far more efficient than anaerobic metabolism.

- Aerobic Metabolism: Oxygen is used in the Krebs cycle (or citric acid cycle) to produce ATP, the energy currency of the cell. Each molecule of glucose metabolized aerobically produces 36-38 molecules of ATP.

- Anaerobic Metabolism: In the absence of sufficient oxygen, cells switch to anaerobic metabolism, which produces far less energy (only 2 ATP per glucose molecule) and generates lactic acid as a byproduct. Elevated lactate levels are a marker of tissue hypoxia and metabolic stress.

Maintaining an adequate supply of oxygen to tissues is critical to ensure efficient energy production. Without sufficient oxygen, cells will shift to anaerobic metabolism, leading to acid-base imbalances and potential cellular injury or death.

Factors Influencing Oxygen Delivery to Tissues

Several factors influence the amount of oxygen delivered to tissues, and healthcare providers must be aware of these when managing oxygen therapy:

- Cardiac Output: The amount of blood the heart pumps per minute (cardiac output) directly impacts oxygen delivery. If cardiac output is low (e.g., in heart failure or shock), oxygen delivery to tissues will be impaired, even if blood oxygen levels are normal.

- Hemoglobin Levels: Oxygen delivery also depends on the amount of hemoglobin available to carry oxygen. Anemia (low hemoglobin levels) reduces the blood's oxygen-carrying capacity, which can lead to tissue hypoxia even if oxygen saturation is normal.

- Oxygen Saturation (SpO2): The percentage of hemoglobin saturated with oxygen must be within a therapeutic range (usually 92-96%) to ensure adequate oxygen delivery. Too low, and tissues will not receive enough oxygen; too high, and there is a risk of oxygen toxicity.

- Peripheral Vascular Resistance: The resistance blood encounters as it flows through the circulatory system affects oxygen delivery. Conditions that cause vasoconstriction (narrowing of blood vessels) can reduce blood flow to tissues, compromising oxygen delivery.

MODULE THREE

LESSON: CLINICAL SIGNS OF OXYGEN DEFICIENCY AND EXCESS

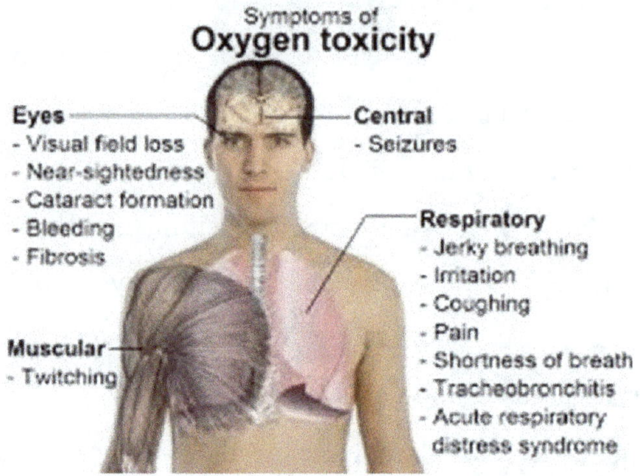

As healthcare providers, the ability to recognize clinical signs of oxygen deficiency (hypoxia) and excess (hyperoxia) is critical in managing patients who require oxygen therapy. The body relies on a delicate balance of oxygen for optimal function, and deviations from this balance can result in significant physiological consequences. In this lesson, we will delve into the clinical manifestations of hypoxia and hyperoxia, their physiological effects, and how to identify these conditions in patients. We will also explore the importance of early detection and prompt intervention to prevent complications.

Understanding Hypoxia: Oxygen Deficiency

Hypoxia occurs when there is insufficient oxygen available to tissues to meet metabolic demands. The condition can arise from several causes, including impaired oxygen delivery, reduced oxygen content in the blood, or a failure of cells to use oxygen effectively. Hypoxia can be classified into different types, each with unique causes and clinical presentations:

- Hypoxemic Hypoxia: The most common form, caused by low arterial oxygen levels (PaO2) due to respiratory issues such as chronic obstructive pulmonary disease (COPD), asthma, pneumonia, or acute respiratory distress syndrome (ARDS). In this type, the oxygen content in the blood is low.

- Anemic Hypoxia: Occurs when there is inadequate hemoglobin available to carry oxygen, despite normal oxygen levels in the lungs. Causes include anemia, blood loss, or carbon monoxide poisoning, which displaces oxygen on hemoglobin molecules.

- Stagnant (Circulatory) Hypoxia: Occurs when oxygen delivery is reduced due to poor blood flow, as seen in conditions like heart failure, shock, or circulatory collapse. Even with normal oxygen levels in the blood, tissues may not receive enough oxygen due to impaired circulation.

- Histotoxic Hypoxia: Occurs when cells are unable to use oxygen effectively, despite adequate oxygen delivery. This is typically caused by poisoning, such as cyanide poisoning, which inhibits cellular respiration.

Clinical Signs of Hypoxia

Recognizing the clinical signs of hypoxia early is essential for timely intervention. Hypoxia can present with a variety of symptoms, depending on its severity and the underlying cause. These signs can range from subtle to severe and include both systemic and localized manifestations:

- Cyanosis: A bluish discoloration of the skin, lips, and mucous membranes is one of the most recognizable signs of hypoxia. It results from the deoxygenation of hemoglobin, leading to darker blood that causes a bluish hue, especially visible in the extremities and around the mouth.

- Tachypnea: Rapid breathing (tachypnea) is an early response to hypoxia, as the body attempts to increase oxygen intake. In severe cases, respiratory distress may occur, characterized by labored breathing, use of accessory muscles, and nasal flaring.

- Tachycardia and Hypertension: The heart compensates for low oxygen levels by increasing cardiac output, leading to an elevated heart rate (tachycardia) and, initially, higher blood pressure (hypertension). If hypoxia persists, it may lead to hypotension as the heart becomes overworked and unable to maintain blood pressure.

- Altered Mental Status: Hypoxia can cause confusion, agitation, restlessness, and difficulty concentrating. As oxygen deprivation worsens, patients may experience disorientation, lethargy, or even loss of consciousness. Severe hypoxia can lead to coma if left untreated.

- Fatigue and Weakness: Oxygen is essential for energy production, so hypoxia often results in generalized fatigue, muscle weakness, and a sense of exhaustion, even with minimal exertion.

- Dizziness and Headaches: The brain is highly sensitive to oxygen levels, and even mild hypoxia can lead to symptoms such as dizziness, lightheadedness, and headaches. These signs are common in conditions like high-altitude sickness, where oxygen levels in the atmosphere are reduced.

- Decreased Urine Output: Hypoxia can lead to reduced kidney perfusion, resulting in decreased urine output (oliguria) as the body prioritizes blood flow to vital organs like the heart and brain.

- Arrhythmias and Chest Pain: The heart muscle is particularly sensitive to oxygen deprivation. Hypoxia can result in abnormal heart rhythms (arrhythmias) and angina (chest pain), particularly in patients with underlying heart conditions.

Degrees of Hypoxia

Hypoxia can range in severity from mild to life-threatening. The following classifications help guide clinical decision-making:

- Mild Hypoxia: Patients may exhibit subtle signs, such as mild tachycardia, anxiety, and restlessness. Pulse oximetry readings may show oxygen saturation levels between 90-94%. Immediate intervention with low-flow oxygen therapy can usually correct this condition.

- Moderate Hypoxia: Signs become more apparent, including confusion, cyanosis, tachypnea, and tachycardia. Oxygen saturation levels fall between 85-89%. Moderate hypoxia requires prompt oxygen supplementation and careful monitoring of the patient's respiratory and cardiovascular status.

- Severe Hypoxia: This is a medical emergency characterized by altered mental status, cyanosis, respiratory distress, and arrhythmias. Oxygen saturation levels are typically below 85%. Immediate high-flow oxygen, ventilatory support, and aggressive treatment of the underlying cause are required.

Hyperoxia: Oxygen Excess

While hypoxia is a common concern, healthcare providers must also be aware of the risks of hyperoxia excessive oxygen levels in the blood. While oxygen is necessary for life, too much oxygen can be harmful, particularly in certain patient populations, such as those with chronic lung disease or critically ill patients in the ICU.

Pathophysiology of Hyperoxia

Hyperoxia occurs when arterial oxygen levels (PaO2) are excessively high, usually due to the administration of high concentrations of supplemental oxygen. While hyperoxia can improve oxygenation in the short term, prolonged exposure to high oxygen levels can lead to oxidative stress, lung injury, and other complications. The body produces reactive oxygen species (ROS) in response to high oxygen levels, which can damage cellular membranes, proteins, and DNA.

Clinical Signs of Hyperoxia

- Cough and Respiratory Discomfort: Patients receiving high concentrations of oxygen for prolonged periods may experience irritation of the airways, leading to coughing, a sore throat, and chest discomfort.

- Oxygen Toxicity: Prolonged exposure to high concentrations of oxygen (typically $FiO2 > 60\%$) can lead to oxygen toxicity, characterized by damage to the lungs. This can manifest as pulmonary edema (fluid buildup in the lungs), atelectasis (collapse of lung tissue), or even acute respiratory distress syndrome (ARDS).

- Central Nervous System (CNS) Effects: Hyperoxia can affect the CNS, leading to symptoms such as headache, dizziness, nausea, and visual disturbances. In severe cases, hyperoxia can cause seizures, particularly in patients with underlying neurological conditions.

- Retinopathy of Prematurity (ROP): In neonates, particularly premature infants, hyperoxia can cause a condition known as retinopathy of prematurity, where abnormal blood vessels grow in the retina, leading to vision problems and potential blindness.

- Reduced Respiratory Drive: In patients with chronic lung diseases, particularly COPD, the body's primary drive to breathe is based on low oxygen levels rather than elevated carbon dioxide levels (CO_2). Administering high levels of oxygen in these patients can suppress their respiratory drive, leading to hypoventilation, CO_2 retention, and respiratory failure.

Prevention of Hyperoxia

To prevent hyperoxia, healthcare providers must carefully titrate oxygen therapy to achieve the lowest effective dose that maintains adequate oxygenation. Monitoring oxygen saturation levels via pulse oximetry and arterial blood gases is essential to ensure patients do not receive excessive oxygen.

- Target Oxygen Saturation: For most patients, oxygen saturation levels between 92-96% are sufficient to meet tissue oxygen demands. For patients with COPD or other chronic lung conditions, lower targets (88-92%) may be appropriate to avoid hyperoxia and CO_2 retention.

- Weaning Oxygen Therapy: Once patients are stabilized, it is important to wean them off supplemental oxygen as soon as possible. Continuous monitoring ensures that oxygen levels remain within the therapeutic range without causing harm.

MODULE FOUR

LESSON: DIAGNOSTIC IMAGING IN OXYGEN THERAPY: UNDERSTANDING X-RAY AND OTHER MODALITIES

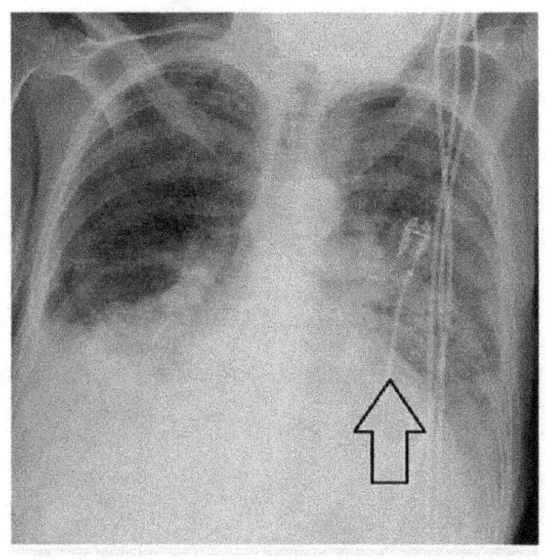

Diagnostic imaging plays an essential role in the management of patients receiving oxygen therapy. Imaging modalities such as chest X-rays, computed tomography (CT) scans, and other diagnostic tools help healthcare providers assess the effects of oxygen therapy, identify complications, and monitor the progression or improvement of underlying diseases. In thislesson, we will focus on how these imaging techniques are used to evaluate the lungs and other organs in patients receiving oxygen therapy, and how to interpret these images to inform clinical decision-making.

Chest X-ray: A Key Tool in Oxygen Therapy

The chest X-ray (CXR) is the most commonly used imaging modality in the assessment of patients receiving oxygen therapy. It is a quick, non-invasive, and widely available tool that provides valuable information about the status of the lungs, heart, and surrounding structures. Healthcare providers rely on chest X-rays to monitor conditions such as pneumonia, pulmonary edema, atelectasis, and other complications related to oxygen therapy.

Indications for Chest X-rays in Oxygen Therapy

Chest X-rays are typically ordered when there is concern about respiratory function or when complications from oxygen therapy are suspected. Common indications include:

- Acute Respiratory Distress: In patients who are experiencing sudden worsening of respiratory symptoms, a chest X-ray can help determine whether conditions such as pneumonia, pulmonary edema, or atelectasis are contributing to the problem.

- Persistent Hypoxia: If a patient remains hypoxic despite receiving oxygen therapy, a chest X-ray may help identify the underlying cause, such as a collapsed lung, fluid buildup, or an infectious process.

- Monitoring Progression of Disease: In patients with chronic respiratory conditions such as COPD or interstitial lung disease, chest X-rays can help assess disease progression and the response to oxygen therapy or other treatments.

- Identifying Complications of Oxygen Therapy: High concentrations of oxygen can cause lung injury over time. Chest X-rays are used to monitor for signs of oxygen toxicity, such as pulmonary fibrosis or barotrauma (damage to the lungs caused by excessive pressure).

Key Findings on Chest X-rays

Chest X-rays provide a wealth of information that can guide the management of oxygen therapy. Some of the key findings that healthcare providers should look for include:

- Increased Lung Opacity (Consolidation): Areas of increased opacity on a chest X-ray suggest the presence of fluid, infection, or inflammation within the lung tissue. This can be seen in conditions like pneumonia, where the alveoli are filled with pus or other inflammatory material.

- Pulmonary Edema: Pulmonary edema, or the accumulation of fluid in the lungs, often appears as a diffuse, bilateral "fluffy" pattern on a chest X-ray. It can be caused by heart failure or fluid overload, and it may be exacerbated by excessive oxygen administration, especially in vulnerable patients.

- Atelectasis: Atelectasis refers to the collapse of lung tissue, which may result from prolonged bed rest, shallow breathing, or mucus plugging. On a chest X-ray, atelectasis may appear as areas of increased density, with the affected lung tissue pulling towards the hilum (central area of the lungs).

- Pneumothorax: A pneumothorax occurs when air enters the space between the lung and the chest wall, causing the lung to collapse. This can happen spontaneously or as a result of trauma or barotrauma from mechanical ventilation or oxygen therapy at high pressures. On a chest X-ray, a pneumothorax appears as an area without lung markings, with the edge of the collapsed lung visible.

- Interstitial Changes (Fibrosis): Prolonged exposure to high concentrations of oxygen can cause lung damage, resulting in interstitial changes such as fibrosis. On a chest X-ray, this may appear as diffuse, fine reticular (network-like) opacities, often referred to as a "ground-glass" appearance. These changes suggest chronic lung injury and can be seen in patients with oxygen toxicity.

- Pleural Effusion: Pleural effusion, or the accumulation of fluid in the pleural space (the area between the lung and the chest wall), appears as a homogeneous opacity in the lower parts of the chest. This can be caused by heart failure, infection, or malignancy and may contribute to respiratory compromise in patients on oxygen therapy.

- Cardiomegaly: Enlargement of the heart, or cardiomegaly, may be visible on a chest X-ray, particularly in patients with heart failure. Cardiomegaly can lead to pulmonary congestion and increased pressure in the lungs, exacerbating hypoxia.

Computed Tomography (CT) Scans

While chest X-rays provide a quick snapshot of lung status, CT scans offer a more detailed and comprehensive view of the lungs, airways, and surrounding structures. CT scans are particularly useful when chest X-rays do not provide enough information to explain a patient's symptoms, or when more detailed imaging is needed to assess the severity of lung disease.

Indications for CT Scans

CT scans are often used in the following situations:

- Unexplained Respiratory Symptoms: If a patient's clinical condition does not improve with oxygen therapy, and a chest X-ray does not reveal the cause, a CT scan can provide more detailed imaging to help identify the underlying problem.

- Suspected Pulmonary Embolism: A CT pulmonary angiogram (CTPA) is the gold standard for diagnosing pulmonary embolism, a life-threatening condition where a blood clot blocks one of the pulmonary arteries. Pulmonary embolism can cause sudden hypoxia and respiratory distress, and a CT scan can help confirm the diagnosis.

- Assessment of Interstitial Lung Disease: In patients with suspected or known interstitial lung disease, a high-resolution CT (HRCT) scan can provide detailed images of the lung parenchyma, allowing for a more accurate assessment of fibrosis, honeycombing, and other changes associated with chronic lung conditions.

- Detection of Tumors or Masses: CT scans can help identify and characterize lung tumors, nodules, or other masses that may be causing respiratory symptoms. This is particularly important in patients with a history of smoking or other risk factors for lung cancer.

MODULE FIVE

LESSON: TREATMENT PROTOCOLS IN ADVANCED OXYGEN THERAPY

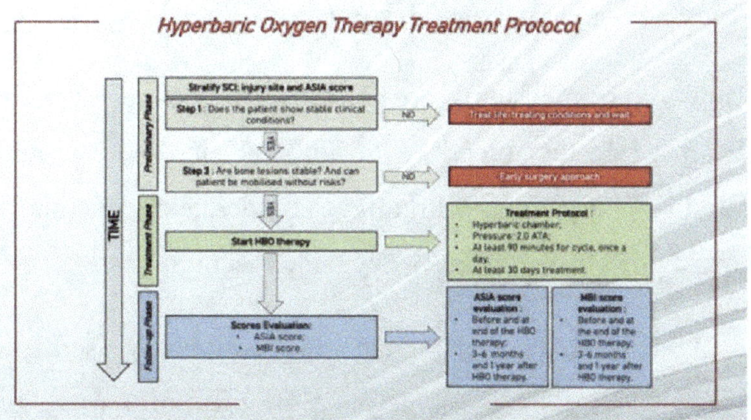

Oxygen therapy is an essential intervention for patients experiencing respiratory distress or hypoxia. However, its application requires a structured approach, especially in advanced settings where the patient's condition may be critical, and a high degree of precision is necessary. This lesson delves into the treatment protocols for advanced oxygen therapy, including the types of oxygen delivery systems, appropriate oxygen flow rates, medications used in conjunction with oxygen therapy, and the role of ventilatory support.

1. Principles of Oxygen Delivery

The primary goal of oxygen therapy is to maintain adequate oxygenation of tissues and organs without causing harm, such as oxygen toxicity or hyperoxia. Effective oxygen therapy begins with selecting the appropriate delivery method and adjusting the flow of oxygen to match the patient's needs. The method of oxygen delivery depends on several factors, including the patient's oxygen saturation, underlying disease, and level of consciousness.

Low-Flow Oxygen Delivery Systems

Low-flow oxygen systems are designed to deliver supplemental oxygen at a rate that blends with ambient air. These systems are typically used for patients with mild to moderate hypoxemia who do not require precise control over oxygen concentrations.

- Nasal Cannula: This is the most commonly used low-flow device. It delivers oxygen at flow rates of 1 to 6 liters per minute (L/min), which corresponds to an FiO2 (fraction of inspired oxygen) of 24-40%. Nasal cannulae are comfortable, easy to use, and well-tolerated by patients who are awake and breathing spontaneously.

- Simple Face Mask: A face mask is used when higher oxygen concentrations are needed. It can deliver oxygen at 5 to 10 L/min, corresponding to an FiO2 of 40-60%. It is useful for patients who require more oxygen than a nasal cannula can provide but do not need precise control over oxygen delivery.

- Reservoir Masks: These masks, such as the non-rebreather mask (NRB), include a reservoir bag that holds oxygen, allowing for delivery of higher FiO2 (up to 100%). They are used for patients in severe respiratory distress who require high concentrations of oxygen. Flow rates typically range from 10 to 15 L/min.

High-Flow Oxygen Delivery Systems

High-flow oxygen systems are designed to deliver a precise concentration of oxygen, which is particularly important in critically ill patients. These systems reduce the risk of rebreathing exhaled gases and provide better control over oxygenation.

- Venturi Mask: This device uses a valve to mix oxygen with room air, allowing for precise control of FiO2 (ranging from 24% to 60%). It is commonly used in patients with chronic obstructive pulmonary disease (COPD) or other conditions where accurate oxygen delivery is important to avoid hyperoxia.

- High-Flow Nasal Cannula (HFNC): HFNC systems can deliver a high flow of oxygen (up to 60 L/min) at precisely controlled concentrations. The humidified and heated oxygen reduces the risk of airway dryness and improves patient comfort. HFNC is useful in managing patients with respiratory failure, especially those who may otherwise require non-invasive ventilation.

Oxygen Monitoring and Titration

Continuous monitoring of oxygen saturation using pulse oximetry (SpO2) is essential to guide adjustments in oxygen therapy. The target oxygen saturation range depends on the patient's underlying condition:

- General Population: For most patients, an SpO2 of 92-96% is considered adequate.
- COPD or Chronic Lung Disease: In patients with chronic hypercapnia (elevated CO2 levels), the target SpO2 is usually lower, around 88-92%, to avoid suppressing their respiratory drive and leading to CO2 retention.

Arterial blood gas (ABG) analysis is another important tool for evaluating oxygenation and ventilation status, especially in critically ill patients. ABG provides information on PaO2 (arterial oxygen tension), PaCO2 (carbon dioxide levels), and pH, helping guide decisions about oxygen flow rates and the need for ventilatory support.

2. Medications Used in Oxygen Therapy

In many cases, oxygen therapy alone is not sufficient to address the underlying causes of respiratory distress. Medications are often used in conjunction with oxygen therapy to treat the underlying disease, relieve symptoms, and improve oxygenation.

Bronchodilators

Bronchodilators, such as beta-agonists and anticholinergics, are commonly used in patients with obstructive airway diseases (e.g., asthma, COPD) to open the airways and improve airflow. These medications can be delivered via nebulizers or metered-dose inhalers (MDIs) during oxygen therapy.

- Beta-Agonists: Medications like albuterol and salbutamol work by relaxing the smooth muscles in the airways, allowing them to dilate and improve airflow. These drugs are especially effective in managing acute exacerbations of asthma or COPD.
- Anticholinergics: Drugs like ipratropium work by blocking the action of acetylcholine on the airway muscles, preventing constriction and promoting airway dilation.

Corticosteroids

Corticosteroids are anti-inflammatory drugs that reduce swelling and inflammation in the airways. They are particularly useful in patients with conditions like asthma or COPD, where inflammation contributes to airway narrowing.

- Inhaled Corticosteroids: These medications, such as fluticasone or budesonide, are often used for long-term control of chronic respiratory conditions.
- Systemic Corticosteroids: In severe cases, systemic corticosteroids (e.g., prednisone, methylprednisolone) may be administered orally or intravenously to reduce acute inflammation during exacerbations.

Diuretics

In patients with pulmonary edema (fluid in the lungs), diuretics may be used to remove excess fluid and reduce the workload on the heart. Diuretics, such as furosemide, are commonly used in patients with heart failure who present with fluid overload and hypoxia.

Antibiotics and Antivirals

Infections such as pneumonia can impair oxygenation by filling the alveoli with pus, fluid, or debris, reducing gas exchange. Antibiotics or antivirals are prescribed based on the suspected or confirmed pathogen to treat the underlying infection and improve lung function.

Pulmonary Vasodilators

For patients with pulmonary hypertension or other conditions that restrict blood flow in the lungs, pulmonary vasodilators (e.g., nitric oxide, sildenafil) can be used to relax the pulmonary arteries and improve oxygenation by enhancing blood flow to well-ventilated areas of the lung.

3. Non-Invasive Ventilatory Support

For patients who are not able to maintain adequate oxygenation with supplemental oxygen alone, non-invasive ventilatory support may be required. Non-invasive ventilation (NIV) delivers positive pressure to the airways without the need for intubation. It is an important step before considering invasive mechanical ventilation.

Continuous Positive Airway Pressure (CPAP)

CPAP is a mode of non-invasive ventilation that delivers a constant level of positive pressure to keep the airways open during both inhalation and exhalation. CPAP is commonly used in patients with obstructive sleep apnea (OSA), but it is also beneficial in patients with acute pulmonary edema or exacerbations of COPD.

Bi-Level Positive Airway Pressure (BiPAP)

BiPAP provides two levels of positive pressure: a higher pressure during inhalation and a lower pressure during exhalation. This makes it easier for patients to exhale while still receiving enough pressure to keep the airways open. BiPAP is often used in patients with COPD exacerbations, acute respiratory failure, or neuromuscular disorders affecting breathing.

Indications for Non-Invasive Ventilation

Non-invasive ventilation is indicated in patients who are experiencing respiratory distress but who are still able to protect their airway and have a functional respiratory drive. It is commonly used in the following situations:

- Exacerbations of COPD: BiPAP is highly effective in reducing the work of breathing and improving gas exchange in patients with acute exacerbations of COPD.

- Acute Cardiogenic Pulmonary Edema: CPAP can improve oxygenation and reduce the need for intubation in patients with heart failure who present with pulmonary edema.

- Hypoxic Respiratory Failure: NIV can be used to treat patients with mild to moderate hypoxic respiratory failure who are not improving with oxygen therapy alone.

4. Invasive Mechanical Ventilation

In cases where non-invasive ventilation is not sufficient to maintain oxygenation and ventilation, patients may require invasive mechanical ventilation. This involves intubating the patient and connecting them to a ventilator that controls breathing.

Indications for Mechanical Ventilation

Invasive mechanical ventilation is indicated in patients with severe respiratory failure, particularly when there is:

- Inability to Maintain Airway: Patients who are unable to protect their airway due to altered mental status or neuromuscular weakness may require intubation.

- Severe Hypoxia or Hypercapnia: When oxygenation cannot be maintained with non-invasive methods, mechanical ventilation allows for better control of oxygen delivery and removal of CO_2.

- Exhaustion or Respiratory Muscle Fatigue: Patients with respiratory muscle fatigue from conditions like ARDS or

COPD may require ventilatory support to reduce the work of breathing and prevent respiratory collapse.

Ventilator Settings

Once a patient is intubated, the ventilator settings must be carefully adjusted based on the patient's needs. Key parameters include:

- FiO_2: The fraction of inspired oxygen is adjusted to maintain appropriate oxygenation levels without causing oxygen toxicity.

- Positive End-Expiratory Pressure (PEEP): PEEP helps keep the alveoli open at the end of expiration, improving oxygenation and reducing the risk of atelectasis.

- Tidal Volume and Respiratory Rate: These settings are adjusted to match the patient's ventilatory needs and prevent lung injury.

CONCLUSION

This book has explored the intricate and critical role of advanced oxygen therapy in respiratory care. From understanding the physiological underpinnings of oxygen delivery and the clinical signs of hypoxemia, to mastering the application of various oxygen delivery systems, healthcare providers have been equipped with the knowledge needed to manage patients with respiratory failure effectively.

We have discussed the importance of individualized oxygen therapy plans, the need for continuous monitoring, and the significance of patient education and adherence to improve outcomes. The integration of oxygen therapy into comprehensive respiratory care, in collaboration with a multidisciplinary team, ensures that patients receive holistic and optimal treatment.

As healthcare providers continue to face new challenges in treating respiratory illnesses, this book serves as a valuable guide to delivering safe, effective, and compassionate care through advanced oxygen therapy. The knowledge gained here can help clinicians improve patient outcomes, reduce complications, and enhance the quality of life for individuals living with respiratory conditions.

REFERENCES

- American Thoracic Society. (2020). *Clinical Practice Guidelines on Home Oxygen Therapy for Adults with Chronic Lung Disease. American Journal of Respiratory and Critical Care Medicine,* 202(2), 51-62.

- Barach, A. L. (2021). *Oxygen Therapy: Historical Developments and Current Practice. Respiratory Care.*

- Beers, M. H., & Berkow, R. (2019). *The Merck Manual of Diagnosis and Therapy (20th ed.). Merck Research Laboratories.*

- Carlin, B. W., & Wiles, K. (2018). *Portable Oxygen in Chronic Lung Disease: Practical Considerations for Clinical Use. Respiratory Care Clinics of North America.*

- Celli, B. R., & MacNee, W. (2020). *Standards for the Diagnosis and Treatment of Patients with COPD: A Summary of the ATS/ERS Position Paper. European Respiratory Journal*